Here's what readers are saying about

Wakening Your Worth:

"Powerful","Transformational", "Courageous!",

"Feeling the love!"

"Debbie reveals her true-life experiences and wears her heart on her sleeve. She shares her storystep by step and reveals powerful tools and methods for you to shift and transform guilt, shame and fear into worthiness and positivity for moving forward!"

~Kim Somers Egelsee

Multi #1 BestSelling Author and Confidence Expert

"I just finished this book. I love the interactive writing and healing that has been incorporated. You can feel the love and the healing that this book will bring for you. Thank you for writing this and sharing your gifts."

~Anita Salazar

Secretary/Treasurer DCWi

"POWERFUL!!! Thank you for going on this courageous adventure of reliving, healing and writing your story so all of us can heal on our own level. This is my new nightstand "go to" book that helps me change my perception in many situations. I open this book and feel your supportive energy and love, making it safe to go those deep, dark and uncomfortable places where 'True Transformation' occurs. Cheers to you Debbie, fabulous book!"

~Maryann Mullahy

Ultimate Freedom Graduate, Reiki Master

"I loved this book! Debbie makes it easy for you to see what patterns you have, like unworthiness, guilt and shame that are running your life. By sharing some of her tough life experiences, you know she's the real deal. The way you can relate to her, and what she offers, helps you to move through what's not working for you!"

~Bethany Schrader

TV Host, Life Transformed Coach

"In a step by step format, Debbie bravely shares her path to self-worth and guides readers into transforming their lives! Leading the way to individual healing and self-actualization, Debbie is, indeed a warrior!"

~Karla Noonan

M.S Human Development and Best-Selling Author

Debbie Espinoza is a beautiful Earth angel with an incredible story of loss, insurmountable challenges, and amazing triumph! She has taken all the lessons she has learned about overcoming one of the most prolific conditions we humans face - unworthiness - and created a powerful workbook designed to guide you out of the darkness of self-judgment and into the light of self-love. Become a Worthiness Warrior by taking the journey laid out in this book.

~Jacqueline VanCampen

Author of *Letters to my Daughter* and Founder of Wise Heart Within

WAKENING YOUR WORTH

YOUR JOURNEY TO UNLOCKING THE WORTHINESS WARRIOR WITHIN

DEBBIE SHUMAN ESPINOZA

This book is for my children Tyler, Rachel and Hunter. Thank you for never giving up on me, for supporting me and loving me through all of our struggles. I love you with all of my being and would not be the woman I am today without you.

TABLE OF CONTENTS

Foreword

I have been on what some may refer to as "the path" for a little under a decade. During that time, I have traveled all over the world in search of answers to the simplest, yet sometimes most complex of questions: "Who am I?" and "How do I live the life I know I was born to live?" I have meditated at sacred stone sites, and sat with gurus, and masters from all types of lineages. I have studied Christianity and Shamanism in search of my purpose, seeking meaning and answers.

On this path of enlightenment, self-discovery, self-forgiveness, and self-love, I have been brought to my knees more times than I can count. Reflecting on my personal journey it becomes apparent that the foundational piece to truly creating and living a life you love boils down to one truth: believing you are worthy of doing so.

I have had the honor of sharing space with some of the most enlightened people on the planet, and continue to meet amazing souls along the way. Debbie is one of them. However, when we met just four short years ago, she was a shell of the woman she has become. I have had a front row seat to her personal transformation, and it is absolutely awe inspiring.

Debbie has laid out the processes she has gone through to build the life of her dreams, which I promise you is an absolute gift. As I mentioned previously, I have had a front row seat to her metamorphosis.

When I met Debbie, she was in the early stages of her transformation process to become the woman she is today, and I could tell she was lost, open, but lost. She had gone through agonizing trials and challenges and it showed in her demeanor, in her mistrust of others, and in the metaphorical armor she used to protect herself.

Yet, behind the hard shell, there was a glimpse of light within her attempting to emerge. I did not know her whole story until our friendship began to blossom and until she began to blossom. It is not an exaggeration that I have been witness to her transformation. I will never forget one night when we were sitting in my backyard, working on some things. I felt this interesting energy between us. I felt uncomfortable as I couldn't tell whether she was judging me or was simply curious about what I was saying. I confronted her, and she looked me dead in the eye and said, "I just want to know if you are for real." I did not at first understand what she was stating, but I soon realized, as she continued to talk, that she was incredibly suspicious of all the things of which I spoke regarding the "Universe." Eventually, and over time, she became curious. She started exploring the world of spirituality and began to explore herself.

It has been incredible to have had a front row seat to her personal transformation, and it is awe-inspiring to witness her metamorphosis in bloom like a lotus flower emerging from a muddy swamp. I am honored to be writing the Foreword to her first book, which is a direct product of her profound transformation,

Debbie's journey took twists and turns and took her to different corners of the world. She became, what I can only refer to as "touched", meaning, she was awakened to her Divine Grace - the powerful force in the Universe of which we are all made. She connected to a place even I had not been. I started to see years fall from her face and a sparkle I had never really seen took root. I quite literally watched her entire life change.

Being on this path of self-realization, healing, forgiveness, and worth you often meet other seekers who not all truly walk their talk, but Debbie does. When you read her story, you will soon realize she chose a warrior's life; - a life full of challenges, heartbreak, addiction, pain, and ultimately of dispelling the darkness to reveal her true light. But being a warrior doesn't stop there. A true warrior takes her experiences and facilitates others awakening to their own Divine Grace, and an in this case, to their Worthiness Warrior.

Debbie is a thriving warrior who tapped into her self-worth and now wants to help others discover their path to enlightenment.

If you truly desire to be a Worthiness Warrior; someone who knows their true value and what a gift they are to the world, and truly shift your reality, then I recommend reading this book.If you want to transform your life experience, I recommend committing to completing the exercises in this book.If you desire to live the life of your dreams, do the work and cultivate your self-worth.You will soon realize it is your destiny, your birthright to do so.

Amber J. Boswell

International Best-Selling Author, Speaker, and CEO of BEAUTY ALCHEMY

Worthiness

Why do we feel worthy or unworthy?

Worthiness is a self-imposed judgment, a perception of value that we have about ourselves. This perception can either be good or bad. When the perception is good, we feel worthy and when it is bad, we feel unworthy.

All of us have felt the 'bad' perception, or unworthiness at some point in our lives. However, most of us seem to live with this judgment of ourselves on a daily basis. It can keep us from living the lives we deserve and from the relationships we desire, but most of all, it keeps us from truly loving ourselves.

Think back on your life, now focus on the most significant times. The times that stand out to you the most. The times that have had the most impact. During these times when have you felt worthy?_____

_____

_____

_____

_____

_____

_____

_____

What did those moments feel like?

_____

_____

_____

_____

_____

_____

_____

_____

Now, thinking back to those significant times write down the moments in your life when you have felt unworthy.

_____

_____

_____

_____

_____

What did those moments feel like?

_____

_____

_____

_____

_____

_____

_____

_____

_____

_____

_____

_____

_____

_____

_____

_____

_____

_____

For most of us the feelings of unworthiness began in early childhood. As children, we are so open and loving. We believe that the world belongs to us and that we are free. We are free to fearlessly create our own world, feeling that we are special and that our personal light is bright. We believe that we can do, or be anything our hearts desire. Then little by little, people come along and start to chip away at our confidence, our worth, and our light. They say things to us that make us question who we are and the decisions we make.

Can you remember a time when you were little, and you were being your true self in all your glory? Perhaps you were singing, totally unencumbered by others who were watching or maybe you were dancing, pretending to be a prima ballerina doing pirouettes.

.

All you remember is being in that moment of absolute joy and freedom of just being 'you'. Then, you were suddenly jolted by someone telling you to "Stop" or to "Be quiet". Maybe your peers at school or siblings laughed at and made fun of you. Maybe your parents wanted peace and quiet when they were cooking dinner or talking with someone else and then they said something that stung you stopping you in your tracks.

The situation you are remembering might not have even been about you but your perception was that you were doing something wrong or bad. You see children are ego centric, meaning that they think they're causing the things that are happening around them.

The feelings of unworthiness could have started at school, when you thought you were taking too long to learn something, and the teacher made you feel that you were not as smart as the other kids. Any moment in our lives can be a catalyst toward feelings of unworthiness.

Now that you have thought about those times, write them down. Which ones stands out the most?_____

_____

_____

_____

_____

_____

_____

_____

_____

Looking back can you see that those events became defining moments where you started believing that you were 'wrong' simply by being you? These moments are frequently unintentional (except in the cases of abuse) but result from situations in daily life. We hear or observe the actions of others and we decide that we must not be 'good' enough for our critics. These subliminal messages suggest we should change in some way; that who we 'are' is not okay and that we should change to fit in and make others happy with us.

Can you see how this process can cause us to judge ourselves and to look at ourselves as we believe others see us instead of how we were born to see ourselves? The perfection and beauty we are, and were born knowing, slowly gets chipped away piece by piece, and we start to believe the world around us instead of our own heart.

Over time these small or large moments of having someone not truly seeing or accepting us, created a separation in ourselves from who we truly are. This separation is where the judgments form, and the unworthiness starts to take shape in our lives. This pattern continues for the rest of our lives until we do something to change it.

In this book you are going to learn how to change these patterns. Who am I to be the one teaching you this? I am an unworthiness survivor. You see, at the age of 4 my mother left me on a street corner in Santa Monica, CA. She took my older brother with her and I had to walk home and tell my dad she was gone. I was scared and not sure what was happening. She said she would come back to get me in 3 days, but she never returned. Because she was my mom, I loved and trusted her, but she left me devastated. I waited and waited for my mom to come back to me. I cried for her over and over, but nothing changed. She never came. I missed her, and I missed my big brother. Every time the door opened I hoped it was her with my brother and that they were home, but that never happened. After a while, I realized they weren't coming back. At 4 years old what else could I think except that I was not good enough? My brother was good enough, but I wasn't. I thought that maybe if I had been a better little girl, if I had never cried, or made her mad ,if I had been somehow what she wanted, she would have stayed, or at least taken me with her. What did I do wrong that my own mother did not want me?

When you are so hurt and betrayed at such a young age how can you ever feel worthy? The unworthiness I felt from that moment on changed my life forever. It led me down a life of addiction (starting at age 12), promiscuity, prison and the total loss of myself.

My dad was never around, and I lived with friends most of my life. He didn't know how to parent a little girl because he was also an addict. This too, added to my feelings of unworthiness;

first my mom and now my dad did not want me. How could I feel anything but unworthy? My dad tried, but you cannot give what you do not have, and he had the same patterns of unworthiness running in his life as I did. I was the "bad" kid (again more 'wrongness'), always in trouble at school and high on some sort of drug to escape from that pain. The pain was so real. In my eyes, I was not wanted by anyone that I loved.

My first husband was also an addict. I spent years trying to compete with his drugs and to get the love I craved in my soul to fill the gaping hole in my heart. I lost that fight and was left alone again. When I finally found the love of my life at 28, I thought, "Now somebody will stay." I was in what I thought of at the time as the eternal joke of abandonment in my story. One month after our daughter was born he was diagnosed with leukemia. He passed away a year to the day later, leaving me lost and abandoned again, only this time with a newborn. You see, in my life, everyone I loved left me, so I felt I was unworthy of love and most of the time even unworthy of living life at all.

From there, I totally succumbed to my addiction. This went on for years and finally led me to prison where I spent a year from 2010-2011. While in prison, my children were living with a friend whom I had just met. They were so sad and the guilt I felt was overwhelming. How could I do this to my children? What kind of mother was I? The pain I felt for them was unbearable. I cried for them all the time thinking of how scared they must be. You see I knew that pain. I knew what it was like to have my mom there one day and gone the next. I was overcome with feelings that I was just like my mom; abandoning my kids. How could I do to them what had been done to me? I felt like a monster. The thoughts in my head came and went like a tornado swirling all around and I couldn't stop them. But the one thought that kept recurring was that I was NOT my mother, I would never be like her. I would never hurt them the way my mother hurt me. I was not sure how, but I knew that I had to change this pattern forever.

One day while I was in prison, I went down to the church and I fell to my knees, asking God to please take my addictions away, to help me change my life. I knew there had to be a better way to live my life. I made a promise that day, that if he would help me, I would never hurt my children or myself again and that I would change my life.

Since that day I have never again had a craving. My addictions are gone. I swore on that day that my life would change and that I would stay for my children. I knew firsthand how painful abandonment felt and I knew what they were feeling. I never wanted them to experience that again, not for a second and especially not from me, their own mother.

It has not been easy. No change really ever is. When I got out of prison, my children and I were homeless and lived in a tent in my sister's back yard for about 6 months. We have struggled to say the least, but I made a promise to myself that day that am determined to never break. I have now been clean for 6 years. I have come from being homeless in a tent in my sister's back yard with my 3 kids in 2012, to studying for the last 5 years anything and everything in the personal development field. I studied with Rikka Zimmerman, a Global Leader in Transformation with over 15 years of experience, for a year, leading me to become a life transformed coach and speaker. I was also given the Rising Star award in 2016. I am still going through life and it is still not always easy, but I have found the tools to help me heal. My current partner and father of my youngest son is very ill but through my education and healing, I no longer feel that these circumstances are being done "to" me, but know they are all "for" me and for my growth. I am now a voice of inspiration to help others realize they can change the love they feel for themselves as well, that they too, can feel the worth they were born knowing.

It has taken me 47 years and a lot of hard work to become the "Worthiness Warrior" that I am today. I have learned through my hardships that my life has unfolded in total perfection to lead me on the journey I was meant to explore, for me to now help others from a place of experience. I have come from the depths of such unworthiness that I didn't know how to get out of. I just knew I couldn't continue the way I was anymore. I now love myself so much that no matter what happens in my life, I know I am worthy. Nobody can take this away from me.

I am now on a mission to help others claim their worth; to love themselves so fully that the perceptions of others can never change their perception of themselves again.

So…. Let's get started.

Wrongness

When we feel unworthy, the underlying factor is that we feel WRONG. Feelings of unworthiness and wrongness go hand in hand. This too starts in childhood.

Every time we were told by someone to stop being who we were, we were made 'wrong'. That little child in us did not know why we were told to "Stop", or to "Be quiet." All we knew is that we were wrong for what we were doing or being. We figured if our behavior had been right, then nobody would have wanted us to change.

This is where the 'wrongness' of who we are begins. When we are always feeling wrong, on some level, we compensate by looking for acceptance. We start to give up who we know we are in order to not be wrong and to be accepted. If we are accepted, we are approved of, and therefore, not wrong. This becomes a vicious cycle.

But guess what? You have never been wrong! No, not ever! Your life has been pure perfection!

Think about it for a minute. If your life could have been any different, it would have been. Those choices led you to where you are today; to heal your wounds and return to the love and worth you were born with. The choices you made in that moment of time were the ones you knew how to make. You were doing the best you could with what you knew and were in perfect alignment with what the Universe had planned for you and your life's journey, bringing you to the place where you know you are whole and perfect. You are an incredible gift that has, and always will be, worthy of more than you could ever dream of. When we make ourselves 'wrong', we are in disagreement with the Universe. When you make yourself 'wrong', you are questioning the perfection of the Universe itself.

Whatever higher power you believe in, be it God, Source, Buddha, or Universe, do you think It could ever be wrong? No, of course not. This is because the Universe is pure perfection in every way. It knows what It is doing at all times. (We will use the term 'Universe' in this book going forward as I feel it is the most universal).

We will never be able to comprehend with our human minds what divine perfection we were created with. You see, we ARE all ONE with our creator. We are a part of our creator. We can never be wrong because there is no such thing as 'wrongness'. There is only the pure perfection of the Universe.

'Wrongness' is just an illusion, a man-made judgment. The Universe is never wrong, and we are part of the Universe created by the Universe, therefore we cannot be wrong.

However, there are pieces of us that do not know the totality of truth that comes from that statement. This is the part of us that is trapped in the illusion of the little child that became afraid and 'wrong'.

Let's teach that little one inside us that they were never wrong, that nothing has ever been their fault and that there was never a time when they should have done something different. The little one inside us is the perfection of the Universe.

It is time to get into agreement with the Universe to know you have never, can never and will never, be wrong!

Exercise –

A. Get in front of the mirror. Look into your own beautiful eyes. Connect with your inner child, that internal little child inside of you that has been stuck in these moments of 'wrongness'. Now, recall that part of him/her that feels so sad and so 'wrong'.

B. As you look into the mirror, say your name and ask your little one what they feel they have done wrong. Example – "Dearest Debbie, what is it that you think you have done wrong?" Let your little one speak, no matter what is coming up, let it come, do not hold back. Your little one has been held back and unheard for far too long. It is time to release all of that now. Your little one wants to be heard.

C. After you have finished with what you think you have done wrong, tell them how much you love them, how what they did was actually amazing. Tell that little one that you actually approve of what they did and that you are so proud of them that their action was actually perfect because it brought you to exactly where you are today.

D. Now ask your little one, "How does the Universe see this?" Say out loud, "I agree with the Universe that this was not wrong, that I am not wrong. I have never been wrong. This was beautiful and perfect just like the Universe."

E. Continue this exercise daily/weekly until your little one has been through every situation in which they believed they were wrong.

F. Make sure you do not end this exercise until your little one is feeling fully loved and there is no 'wrongness' left around each action they originally perceived as wrong.

G. Feel free to substitute the word 'Universe' for whatever higher power you believe in. This exercise is for you and is between you and your little one with the perfections of your higher power.

Notes

Shame

We all have it!

Nobody wants to talk about it!

The less you talk about it the more it exists!

Shame is defined as:

"The intensely painful feeling or experience of believing that we are flawed and therefore unworthy of love and belonging."-Brene Brown

Shame is a feeling or emotion, unlike worth and self-esteem which are actually judgments and thoughts. We feel shame and think worth.

'Shame' is a huge key in knowing our true worth. If we are living in shame we think that "we" are a mistake, not that what we have done was a mistake, but that "we" are actually the mistake, that our very being is wrong. Shame can come from just a single experience that ripples out through our entire lives.

Example: When my mom left me at such a young age, I had so many "thoughts" of what was wrong with me and what did I do wrong?

After years of these thoughts swirling around in my head I had finally had enough and tried to take the pain away with drugs and sex. These actions made me hate myself. So, the thoughts turned to feelings of how awful "I" was for the things "I" was doing. Not that the "actions" were wrong but that "I" was awful and wrong. Do you see the difference?

I thought that I was totally alone in my pain. From my perspective everyone around me had great families and they all definitely had a mom who loved them. So, my shame just kept growing.

Unspoken shame is very dangerous because continuous feelings of shame become detrimental to self-worth. Shame has been called the "Mother Emotion". It calls into question our very ability to be in connection with others and our response to shame is actually the same as our response to trauma. It is a threat to our being loved and connected.

There are 4 main categories that are tied to shame and understanding these can be very beneficial in understanding where we are.

1. Shame – A focus on self.
2. Guilt – A focus on behavior.
3. Humiliation – A focus on deserving.
4. Embarrassment – A fleeting focus.

Shame and guilt are the two that seem to be most tied together and they are also confused with each other the most. So, let us take a look at each one.

Shame – I am somebody I do not want to be. I "am" a mistake. For example: We feel that we are the problem and that we are 'wrong' as a person.

Write down the last time you felt shame.
What happened? Write how the experience made
you feel.

._____

_____

_____

_____

_____

_____

_____

_____

_____

_____

_____

Guilt – I have done something that does not
match my values or who I want to be. I "have
made" a mistake, that the action I took was a
mistake.

Write down the last time you felt guilty.
What happened? Write how the experience made
you feel.

_____

_____

_____

_____

_____

_____

_____

_____

_____

_____

_____

Humiliation – This correlates with our
feelings of 'deserving'. For example, if we get
angry about a situation and know we did not

deserve it. We don't believe we deserve humiliation, but we believe we deserve our shame.

Write down the last time you felt humiliated. What happened? Write how the experience made you feel.

_____

_____

_____

_____

_____

_____

_____

_____

_____

_____

Embarrassment – This is a fleeting emotion. This is where we know we are not alone, that what has occurred has definitely happened to others. It is also easily laughed off.

Write down the last time you felt embarrassed. What happened? How did the experience make you feel?

_____

_____

_____

_____

_____

_____

_____

_____

_____

_____

_____

Now that we can see the differences, we can see how 'shame' is an attack on our very being and who we are at our core. The good part is that shame only works when we believe we are alone in that pain. The moment we reach out and talk about what we are experiencing, shame can no longer hold on.

This is exactly how I was released from the shame I felt my whole life. It was extremely difficult, and I thought that people would judge me as being bad but quite the opposite actually occurred .I found that I was met with love and compassion. Others were able to empathize with me. There were so many people who were actually proud of me for saying all the things I was ashamed of. This turned shame on its head because it led to feelings of strength knowing I was no longer alone. The truth is, I was never alone. I was just too stuck in my shame to see it.

Let's clear these places deep within us where all our shame is hidden. We have all done things we are ashamed of, and feel bad about ourselves for doing. We are harder on ourselves than anyone else could ever be.

Exercise 1–

Ok, let's recall what you wrote about the last time you remember feeling shame. What occurred during that time?

_____

_____

_____

_____

_____

_____

_____

_____

_____

_____

_____

_____

Can you think back even further and relate this to a time when you were a young child? Write this down.

_____

_____

_____

_____

_____

_____

_____

_____

_____

_____

_____

Are there similarities here? Do these similarities create a pattern that echoes throughout your life? Are you ashamed of them? Yes?

Ok, it is now time to heal this.

Exercise 2-

A. Get in front of the mirror. Look into your own beautiful eyes. Connect with your inner child; now recall that part of him/her that feels ashamed.

B. Go as deep as you can. Really go deep into that time. What are your surroundings like, the air, the smells etc. Remember everything.

C. How old are you?

D. Will you let that _____ year old little one talk now?

E. How does this _____year old feel?

Examples of what feelings may come up: Hurt, sad, scared, unworthy, abandoned, broken, damaged, disappointed, angry, unsafe or just plain wrong.

F. What does your little one need to say about what he/she did?

G. Take 3 deep breaths and release all of this shame.

H. Talk to your little one now. Let them hear you say that they have nothing to be ashamed of. Give them all the love that they need. Have a conversation with them.

Example –"I am so sorry, Debbie that you have been feeling this way, It must be so hard for you to feel like you have done so much that is wrong." Have compassion for this part of you and tell him/her everything they need to hear to heal these deep wounds.

Example- "Debbie, sweetheart, you have done NOTHING to be ashamed of. I am so sorry you have held on to this for so long. I love you so much. Everyone makes mistakes, but YOU are NOT a mistake."

I. Take 3 more deep cleansing breaths. Breathe in this new energy.

J. Use this exercise anytime you feel shame creeping in.

If you can, find a friend that you can talk to about the things you feel ashamed of. Like I said before, shame can only exist if it is in the dark. When we expose it by talking, it can no longer exist.

Notes

<u>Notes</u>

Being Approved of and Accepting Ourselves

Have you ever found yourself trying to prove to someone who you are? Have you ever tried to be who they want you to be, so that you can gain their approval and be accepted?

As for me, I did everything I could to be accepted, to please those around me. I just wanted to be loved and I did not care what I had to do to get that love. What parts of me I had to give up. I did not accept me for my authentic self or approve of any of my choices. I chose to do what others wanted me to do to gain their approval.

You see, our worth is also tied to the perceptions of who and what others think we are. When you are trying to prove yourself, to be accepted by others, you are out of alignment with your true self. You believe somewhere in your core that who you truly are is not good enough. This is your lack of self-worth showing up again.

When this happens, we feel we have to prove we are someone or something we are not in order to gain the love and respect of others.

Ask yourself, "What have you found yourself trying to prove in all the areas your life?"

Write it down.

_____

_____

_____

_____

_____

_____

_____

_____

_____

_____

Do you feel the need to prove to others that you are a good, moral, authentic, or loyal person? Do you give up who you really are to prove this? I am not saying you are NOT these things, but when we try to prove that we are, it literally means we BELIEVE we are not. If you truly believed who you were, you would never have to prove it to anyone to be loved and accepted. You would just be you and those traits would come across naturally without the need for acceptance and approval because YOU would know YOU.

How much of your life have you chosen in order to be accepted and approved of? How much of your life have you lived trying to be accepted by others? Describe those situations in which you 'lost' an authentic part of your core in order to please someone else?

What were the reasons you did this?

What you have described results because there is somewhere in you where you have not fully accepted yourself yet.

When you start to think about the choices you have made, can you think of any that weren't about striving to be accepted or approved of?

Honestly reflect here and write them down in detail.

_____

_____

_____

_____

_____

_____

_____

_____

_____

_____

_____

_____

Were most of the daily choices you made to please someone else? What are some of those?

_____

_____

_____

_____

_____

_____

_____

_____

_____

_____

Were these choices made to prove to yourself that you are a "good" person?

The key to ending this pattern is to ask yourself a few key questions and to finally approve of yourself so you do not search for that approval from others.

Exercise:

Look into the mirror and ask- "What part of me do I not approve of?" There may be quite a lot. Write them down. Be honest and open. The More truthful you are about disapproving of yourself, the more you can clear this pattern.

_____

_____

_____

_____

_____

_____

_____

_____

_____

Where in my life do I find myself doing things I don't really want to do to gain approval? What types of things are they?

_____

_____

_____

_____

_____

_____

_____

_____

_____

Who am I trying to please? Why?

_____

_____

_____

_____

_____

Accepting Ourselves

The reasons we try so hard for approval is that we really do not approve of, or accept ourselves. How can we feel worthy if we do not accept who we are? Ask yourself, "Have I fully accepted me, my life, my past, my present, and maybe even my future for what it truly is?"

Acceptance is a huge step in approving of ourselves and reclaiming our worth. Acceptance doesn't mean that we necessarily agree with something. It means accepting that "it is what it is" and nothing more.

When you are able to accept something just as it is, or was, you are now in alignment with the Universe. All of our life experiences have been created by the Universe to get us into alignment with who we truly are. When we fight what is, and do not accept ourselves and our experiences, we will continue to create the same patterns over and over until we can heal them and bring them into acceptance. Therefore, you must accept you, all of your choices, your past, everything. You must accept everything about you, whether you judged it as good or bad simply doesn't matter. Accepting that it was what happened and that it was perfect for your journey is all that matters.

Exercise –Looking at the Bad/Wrong.

1. What choices have you made that you feel were bad/wrong?

_____

_____

_____

_____

_____

_____

_____

_____

_____

_____

_____

_____

_____

2. What mistakes have you made?

_____

_____

_____

_____

_____

_____

_____

_____

_____

_____

_____

_____

_____

_____

_____

_____

_____

_____

3. What do you wish you could have chosen differently?

_____

_____

_____

_____

_____

_____

_____

_____

_____

_____

_____

_____

_____

_____

_____

_____

4. What in your life have you done that you don't approve of?

_____

_____

_____

_____

_____

_____

_____

_____

_____

_____

_____

_____

_____

_____

Exercise – Looking at the Good/Right

1. What choices have you made that you feel are right/good?

_____

_____

_____

_____

_____

_____

_____

_____

2. What are some great decisions that you have made?

_____

_____

_____

_____

_____

_____

_____

_____

_____

_____

_____

_____

_____

_____

3. What are some decisions that you are
   proud of making?

_____

_____

_____

_____

_____

_____

_____

_____

4. What in your life have you done that you approve of?

_____

_____

_____

_____

_____

_____

_____

_____

_____

_____

_____

_____

Now looking at these wrong/bad, right/good choices, we need to acknowledge and accept them for what they truly are. Those choices were not actually, good or bad or right or wrong. They just were They just happened; that this was the Universe at work in all its perfection. Acknowledge "what is" by saying the truth out loud about each choice you wrote, starting with the bad ones.

1. I know I thought this choice was good/bad, right/wrong in some way, but I am no longer willing to support that belief.

2. I now accept myself and this choice for exactly what it was. It was not good/bad or was not right/wrong it just was.

3. This was exactly what the Universe had planned for me and my journey.

4. There was no other choice I could have made. If I could have chosen something

different, I would have chosen something different.

5. I now fully accept all of my choices for the perfection that they were and are.

6. I now accept me for the perfection that I am.

7. I now accept my past for the perfection that it was

8. I now accept my present moment for the perfection that it is.

9. I now accept my future for the perfection it will be.

I now totally accept ME with every ounce of my being! ALL OF ME! I now know it has all been in perfect alignment with the Universe. Thank you, Universe. Thank you, (_Debbie)_

Notes

Judgments of Ourselves and Others

What are judgments?

Judgments are what we use to suppress the hurt and fear we carry around in our life and this is always a distorted perspective. We use judgment as a way to determine our worthiness or unworthiness, but it is just a judgment we place upon ourselves.

When you judge, you are taking your perspective away from the truth that everything is happening in perfection because judgments are lies. They are the false patterns or programs that rest on top of our deeper hurts.

We use judgments for lots of reasons, but we will look at the two most prevalent. One reason is when we want things to be changed; fixed or improved. An example of this is when you feel unworthy. This is a bad judgment and we want to change, fix or improve how we are feeling or what our circumstance is in the moment. We want the feeling of being unworthy or wrong to go away. We want the circumstance that led to this judgment to be different in some way, in any way. We therefore, want to change, fix or improve the feeling instead of accepting that it is perfect just the way it is and the only thing that needs to change is OUR judgment of it.

The second reason is when we want things to stay the same. When we judge ourselves worthy, we consider this a good thing. We like the feeling or situation and therefore judge it as 'good;' this is wanting things to stay the same. This behavior is usually a subconscious response, but it can occur on a conscious level as well.

Let's look at 'right' judgments first. As I stated before we use 'right' judgments in order to keep things the same. But the Universe is always changing and expanding, so when we judge something as 'right' or 'good' we are limiting the possibilities for something even greater to manifest. You are in essence saying, "I like this, this is right, please keep it the same."How can anything ever change or get better when you are placing a "hold" on where you are and what can actually manifest in your life?

I'll use a relationship as an example. You are in what you call a "good" relationship. You are happy and can't believe how great life is. You are on Cloud 9. Now, something changes, (because it always will. Nothing ever stays the same. The Universe and people are always changing and expanding). Maybe one of you has to work more hours or even loses their job. It now feels different and you feel like you have lost something. Do you see how in your judgment of it being 'good' you actually wanted it to stay the same?

When you use this good/right judgment you are also saying to the Universe, "Do not bring me anything different. "Even though what the Universe had in store for you would be even better. You are cutting off the infinite possibilities of the Universe.

List 5 things in your life right now that you are judging as good.

1._____

_____

_____

_____

_____

2._____

_____

_____

_____

_____

3._____

_____

_____

_____

_____

4._____

_____

_____

_____

5._____

_____

_____

_____

When we are judging something as good/right we also believe subconsciously that the opposite will happen. So, you think that you are judging it as good/right to keep that result, but with that judgment you also believe in bad/wrong. Your consciousness is creating both results simultaneously meaning both results will show up in some form.

Look back at what you wrote as the 5 things you are judging as good/right. For each one name something greater that could manifest if this judgment was not in place.

1._____

_____

_____

_____

2._____

_____

_____

_____

_____

3._____

_____

_____

_____

4._____

_____

_____

_____

5._____

_____

_____

_____

_____

The best way to look at these judgments is to be grateful for what is occurring but be open to what else is possible. I always say that I am open to all the Universe has to offer, be it this or something better. The possibilities are endless.

Bad or wrong judgments are used when we want to change, fix or improve something. When we want it to change we are out of alignment with the Universe and the perfection our life is, and the perfection that we are.

We use bad/wrong judgments to try to avoid something bad/wrong from happening in the future. So, when we are judging ourselves as unworthy we are actually asking the Universe to change and fix us. The Universe knows that we are whole and perfect just the way we are, but will make tools available to us to help us grow and claim the worth we were born with. It is time in your journey for this to happen. That is why you are here reading this book. The Universe is telling you it is time for you to heal and truly love who you are.

The bad/wrong judgments we have also color our experience of life and the world. When this happens, you are unable to experience the pure love that you are. If you judge something as bad/wrong, you will create a bad/wrong experience. In essence when you are judging yourself as unworthy you are creating more unworthiness.

Write down 5 things you have judged as bad or wrong.

1._____

_____

_____

_____

_____

_____

2._____

_____

_____

_____

_____

_____

3._____

_____

_____

_____

_____

_____

4._____

_____

_____

_____

_____

_____

5._____

_____

_____

_____

_____

_____

Where do you think these judgments came from?_____

_____

_____

_____

_____

_____

Guess what? Judgments always come from outside of you. They are NOT yours and self-judgment actually does not exist. There is only what has been projected on to you and what you chose to believe instead of believing in yourself; who you know you truly are.

Say that again!! Self-judgment is what has been projected onto to you and you chose to believe, instead of believing in yourself and who you truly are!

When we judge something, we actually freeze that energy in place.

How would your life feel if you were able to un-judge the bad/wrong energies that have made you feel unworthy and broken?

_____

_____

_____

_____

_____

_____

_____

_____

_____

_____

_____

_____

Where in your life are you trying to be 'right'?

_____

_____

_____

_____

_____

_____

_____

Where in your life do you not want to be 'wrong'?

_____

_____

_____

_____

_____

_____

_____

What other judgments do you have?

_____

_____

_____

_____

_____

_____

_____

Are these judgments real, or just a perspective?

_____

_____

_____

_____

_____

_____

How are these judgments serving you?

_____

_____

_____

_____

_____

_____

_____

_____

Are these judgments actually coming from you or the world around you?

_____

_____

_____

_____

_____

_____

_____

Are you ready to release all of these judgments? Here is how:

1. Commit to yourself that you will stop judging yourself and others.

2. Whenever you feel a judgment coming up or catch yourself judging, picture a STOP sign.

3. Repeat to yourself, –"I did not choose this judgment. This judgment is not my true perspective. I realize that this judgment has nothing to do with the real me."

4. Take 3 deep breaths and release all of the energy of the judgments.

5. If you still feel the judgments, say to yourself – "I am not going to judge myself for judging this. It is ok."

6. Take 3 more deep cleansing breaths.

<u>Notes</u>

Forgiveness

Forgiveness is the biggest hurdle we need to overcome in order to claim our self-worth. When we are unable to forgive (ourselves, others, the Universe or Higher power) we are stuck in the feeling of wrongness. Therefore, when we feel our choices were wrong, or that others have wronged us in some way, we can NOT feel worthy.

When people harm us, it is due to the wrongness that they have placed upon themselves.

They are acting out on to you what has been done to them. They have not forgiven themselves for their past mistakes. This is such a vicious cycle and one of which most people have a hard time understanding the importance. When we are able to forgive ourselves and others this pattern is broken, and we see their pain and have compassion, knowing that this was about them and had nothing to do with us. Forgiving others for what we feel they have "done" to us is so important. When we don't forgive we get stuck in victim mode and think we are unworthy of love and acceptance.

Exercise –

Think of 1 person right now that you feel has done you "wrong". What happened? Write this out in detail, be as descriptive as possible.

_____

_____

_____

_____

_____

_____

_____

_____

_____

_____

_____

_____

_____

_____

_____

_____

_____

_____

_____

Why do you feel that this was wrong? What did it really do to you? Did it hurt your feelings? Did it cause you emotional or physical harm? Were your expectations not met? What is the real reason you feel this was wrong?

_____

_____

_____

_____

_____

_____

_____

_____

_____

_____

_____

_____

_____

_____

What sort of effect did this have on your overall quality of life?

_____

_____

_____

_____

_____

_____

_____

_____

_____

Now, look at this situation again.

Was this occurrence malicious?

Was it a misunderstanding?

Were things not communicated properly?

Did they mean to hurt you?

_____

_____

_____

Finally, can you see where in their life they have been hurt or betrayed in a similar way and that a pattern is just repeating and asking to be healed?_____

It is now time to forgive them.

Take 3 deep breaths, close your eyes and bring up an image of them in your mind. See if you can picture them as the hurt little child they once were when they were hurt and betrayed in the same way.

Open your heart and say out loud, – "I forgive you." _____.

"I know that you did not mean to hurt me. I know that you were only doing to me what has once been done to you. I am willing to send you love, compassion and understanding so that we can heal this pattern together"

I forgive you _____.

I love you _____.

Now, do this for every person you feel has ever wronged you. Include forgiving your higher power and the Universe in this exercise.

That was a huge step and I am so proud of you for being willing to make it. The power of forgiveness is one of the greatest powers of the Universe. It heals EVERYTHING!!

Forgiving oneself seems to be the hardest part for most people. It is much easier, and we are much more willing to forgive others and have compassion for them than we are willing to have compassion for and forgive ourselves.

It is time to forgive yourself for anything that you feel you have done wrong in your life so that you can have a loving, caring and supportive relationship with yourself. When you do, unworthiness can no longer exist because you know you, your choices and your life has been in complete perfection.

We start making ourselves 'wrong' at such an early age. Can you see how these wounds can go back so far and run so deep? When I started the process of forgiving myself I was so scared. This was all so new to me as I was used to pushing all of my feelings away, as deep down inside as I could get them. I had done whatever I could to try to forget them. Now I was supposed to bring them forward. What? This was going to be hard and I was scared. I had to go back so far into my childhood and bring up the deepest places where I had betrayed and hurt myself. I revisited all those deep dark places where I had labeled myself so 'wrong'. It is time for you to do the same.

Exercise –

Close your eyes and take 3 deep cleansing breaths. Now ask yourself, "What is the most shameful thing I have ever done to myself? How have I betrayed myself the most"?

_____

_____

_____

_____

_____

_____

_____

_____

_____

_____

_____

_____

_____

How old are you?

_____

How does this _____year old feel?

_____

_____

_____

_____

_____

_____

_____

_____

What does your _____year old need to say about what he/she did? Let them speak, do not hold anything back.

_____

_____

_____

_____

Wakening Your Worth

Now, let's give that _____ year old love, compassion and understanding.

Start by saying, "(Debbie), I am so sorry you went through this. It must have been so hard for you to betray yourself in this way."

"I Understand how doing this could have made you feel so wrong, but _____ you were not wrong. You were doing the best you could with what you knew at the time".

"I forgive you _____. You are safe now and you never have to betray yourself in this way ever again."

"I love you so much_____ and I know that this has all been perfectly orchestrated by the Universe, so we can heal."

"You are perfect and whole just the way you are. You are forgiven_____."

"There is NOTHING you could ever do that would make me not love you. I will always love you."

Take 3 deep cleansing breaths and allow the forgiveness to flow through your body.

You will need to do this exercise with all of the times you felt you have been wrong and betrayed yourself. Do this until there is no more energy of being wrong coming up around your life.

This is not easy, but I promise you if you do the work I outlined here you will have a new perspective on life. Your self-worth will shine. You will Love who you are. Your life will blossom and the lives of those around you will benefit as well. You will see others as the Love

that they truly are and you will see yourself as the
Love you truly are. The whole effect of
forgiveness opens up a life beyond your wildest
dreams.

Notes

CONCLUSION

I am so honored that you let me be your guide on this journey into reclaiming your worth and truly and fully loving yourself.

There is no greater gift you can give yourself than healing your core wounds, claiming your worth and loving yourself infinitely. Everything in your life is a reflection of your relationship with yourself.

Re-claiming your true worth and value is a process of healing and forgiveness. Knowing that deep down in your core you are worthy of love, you are worthy of forgiveness, you are worthy of self-love and you are worthy of your hearts' desire. You were born worthy. You have always been worthy.

Personal worthiness includes forgiving and respecting yourself and feeling compassion, respect, kindness and appreciation for who were created to be.

By identifying and peeling down the layers of hurt, judgment and pain, you will override them with feelings of love, acceptance and worth. You will know that you are a divine gift, whole and perfect. You will become aligned with who you truly are and who you were meant to be.

When you hold these new beliefs, they become part of you. Believing in your true value and worth you become unshakeable in your love for yourself and your life.

About the Author

Winner of the 2016 Rising Star award, Debbie Shuman Espinoza is the Worthiness Warrior. She is an award-winning Author, Speaker, Life Transformation/Self Love Coach and International Entrepreneur.

She has studied self-help and personal development for over six years; she holds numerous workshops and classes where she speaks and teaches about claiming the worthiness we were born with, and ending the shame we hide.

Debbie has overcome many obstacles in her life, among them the death of her husband when she was just 34, her 35-year addiction to prescription drugs and much more. This has inspired her to become a transformation coach who is passionate about helping others change their lives, triumph over hardships and realize their dreams.

Debbie is a widowed mother of 3 amazing children who have always believed in her and supported her. Because of them and their love, she has been able to reclaim her life and finally realize her potential. She now wants others to know they too can rewrite their story claim their worth and have all they have ever dreamed of.